The Divine Revolution

Elizabeth Ervin

BookLeaf
Publishing

Presentation by *BookLeaf Publishing*

Web: www.bookleafpub.com

E-mail: info@bookleafpub.com

ISBN: 9789357441872

First edition 2023

DEDICATION

Dedicated to all the souls who survived the journey of defenseless heartbreak and surrendered to divine love creating a world of new beginnings.

Inevitable End

People spend most of their human days thinking.
Planning life for the next major step.
We are not ready for the unexpected.
The world is filled with the unexpected.
Death is unexpected but is the only matter one
can expect at the end of all that planning.
We expect it.
We prepare for it.
We understand it.
We all know it is coming.
We are planning to wait for the inevitable end.

The Wall

What is death an end to?
Is it an end to the pain of life's broken promises?
The end of life's joyous rewards?
Are we happy in times of achievement?
Are we happy in times of success?
Are we happy in times of acceptance?
Can we know happiness if we haven't experienced pain?
What if the trick to happiness is knowing enough pain in which happiness is felt when found?
Will we know it?
Can we feel it?
Did we build the wall around it while coping with the trauma?
This is the case as happiness is secured in the soul of our being.
The walls are built.

The Journey Begins

The wall was sealed in trauma.
The bricks laid for us by generational curses or
influences and cemented together by
every…single…act against us.
Sauntered by the lovers who did not love.
We are self-punished for the hearts given in vain.
Given in ignorance.
Solitary confinement for the purpose of
understanding why.
Why did we love in the first place?
How is the next disaster prevented?
We seek to understand.
The journey begins.

The Wall Stands

We test the wall, you know?
We test it by letting weak people in to see what
they can do.
Can they break it?
Will they break it?
They will not.
They will not because it is strong.
It is known to be strong, because it was built by
the architect of our own lives.
The shell for our souls. It was built by us.
Yet, it is tested.

It has become a constant logical evaluation of patterns trending in the mind.
It is a source of data collection.
If one gets past the gate, then one is worthy of seeing what is inside.
If one is a fraud. They are destroyed, like at the beginning of the Trojan war, tempted by beauty and appeal.
They do not get in because the wall stands, and it is protected by the mind.
One does not lose the Trojan war twice.
There will be no more sacrificial distribution of the heart.
The wall stands.

Validation

The test is repeated, like all research and valid study.
The test is used to find the limitations. The weaknesses in logic.
Testing any alternate viewpoint to prove the walls' use, purpose, and placement.
One does this in the naive belief that another will disprove the need for the wall's existence.
Secretly one hopes it is not disproven. The tests continue.
Past patterns indicate that if the wall is destroyed or even-tempered with, an onset of what would be the slaughter to inevitable death of not only the protected, but the intruder will begin.
All will be destroyed.
All will be eliminated.
Pain will cease at the keeper's will and in a controlled environment.
In this dynamic of controlled mind, heart, and soul one is considered strong.
He is successful in the prevention of pain and therefore, the creator of self-achieved happiness.
The keeper of the wall is alone.
Alone is the variable.

How can alone be the source of happiness and
pain at the same time?
Can we even define alone within the wall?
Is alone what we are protecting?
The play on words is puzzling but they are true
within the wall.

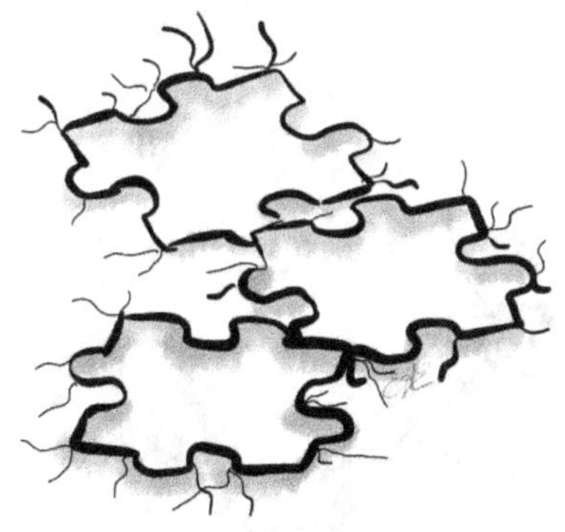

The Battle Begins

As the data is collected there is an occasion
where one breaches the borders.
The person is not present.
They are not real, yet they exist within the wall.
How did they get here?
How was that person missed?
The fortress is greater than any known to man.
Yet here the other soul stands.
It too is dark; it is unclear if it is safe.

It is a filler of the void but how did it get in?
It came from an avenue not of the physical
encounter and bridged its way in via the folds of
the mind and found the heart.
The intricate design between logic and emotion
was a missed maze.
It did not require protection as it was a maze not
even the keeper could untangle.
The new soul brings chaos and peace together.
It is terrifying but safe.
Commence the test plan!
The defense! The fight of wills to survive! The
battle for the space within the wall begins!
There is no victory!
The souls are still there.
The wall stands.

The Breach

How can one breach the code of logic not even
understood by the logic holder?
How can the heart beat for a being it has not touched?
Why does it happen?
How does it happen?
It was not permitted.
It will not be permitted.
The new data has been created.
The new problems must be solved.

The Key

Both souls now reside in the wall.
The journey to find the key to survival has been
embarked on by both now on the inside.
Proving worth to each other they become familiar.
Building a trusted pattern to know each piece is
laid correctly, appropriately, and logically.
The master plan for the survival of happiness on
the path to the inevitable death is newly secured.
This is not an easy task.
It has no right answer.
It has no hints.
There is no search bar or book.
It is a journey unique to the souls within the wall.
Since there is no other existence within the wall
there is no resource.
The answer lies between the keeper and the
intruder.
Trust is the key.

Our Safety

As the new data is slowly decoded, the old research
of securing the wall becomes less critical.
The new data has overtaken the mind that guards the
soul.
The soul is left unarmed but is not being wounded
until it realizes it's not being wounded.
The fight resumes to establish trust.
The cycle is repeated.
The intruder is still unknown as she has not yet
become a physical object.
The intruder slowly becomes safer and safer as she
has yet to pose a real threat.
There is no expectation.
No risk.
No source of physical pain as she has not moved in
any direction within the wall.
She is there only to help him survive the journey.
This is nice.
This is needed.
This is what the wall was for.
We are safe.
We do not feel alone within the wall.

Uncontrolled Reality

The mind is a strange thing.
It tells us how to feel and respond.
Life is a collection of data from experiences that mankind uses to fight or flee in response to stimuli.
When a variable enters that the mind has missed, it becomes turmoil.
It can become a solstice.
That variable is a product of the uncontrolled environment.
Regardless of the wall, the environment is, in fact, uncontrolled.

Her Unknown

The keeper of the wall doesn't realize that the other soul did not know she had entered such territory.
In her own quest for study, the wall was encountered and entered.
Innocently but swiftly.
The maze through the keeper's mind was not easy yet handed out during his test plan as a variable that has failed with other threats.
While data was collected, and connections were made the unsuspecting intruder breached each fold of his mind in search for what made her curious behind the wall in the first place.
He is the unknown in her own study.

Behind His Wall

Behind that wall was a soul the intruder recognized;
he was not a threat.
He presented a challenge.
In the process, the intruder faced reflection, growth,
and the retention of knowledge to understand the
facets of the mind that guards the keeper's soul.
Always, the heart was beating.
What the keeper also does not know is that in the
process of entry, the intruder has realized her own
potential threat.
She left behind her own wall to seek the mystery
behind his.
The keeper was fascinating and sparked like an
electric shock.
He was magnetic.
The intruder was summoned.
He seemed so mysterious. So distant. Yet completely
recognizable.
He is captivating as he tossed out variables of genius
and insanity, together, simultaneously.
He is magnificent.

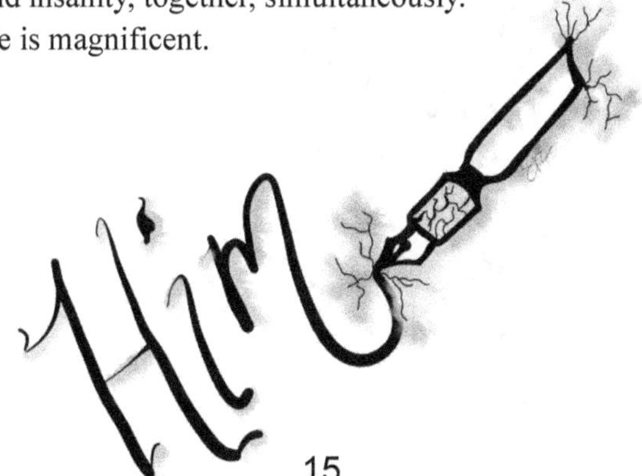

She Stands

The intruder knows the keeper's pain.
She sees his heart instantly.
With a focus on the heart and a method of using a
small light through the dark mind of the keeper, the
intruder made her way in, in peace.
The keeper handed the key to the intruder from the
start.
They spoke the same language.
It was in the music.
The intruder understood and followed the orders of
instruction.
She heard his melody.
She stood securely inside his wall.

The Keeper & His Intruder

The intruder was not an intruder.
She is a peacemaker.
Her soul was masked as dark, but she is his light.
She brought understanding. Acceptance. Kindness.
She is not threatened by hopelessness or
vulnerability.
Still, an intruder is an intruder.
The wall cannot be broken but it has been cracked.
The intruder realizes that not only has she cracked the
keeper's wall, but she has left hers unattended.
In rational thinking and emotionless decision, the
intruder found a way to build a new barrier for herself
using the tools provided in her original study.
She must lay down her sword.
The intruder does not want to hurt the keeper.
The keeper is good.
The keeper is safe.
She surrenders.

The Shield

A plan is devised to protect both inhabitants of the wall.
The plan is implemented.
The threats have been eliminated.
They are no longer alone but not physically together.
This is now their shield for each other.
They have found something outside of either logic or
emotions.
It is understanding.
It is unconditional.
It is simple existence.
It is the act of being alone with another for an unknown
period of time but poses no harm to the now joint keepers
of the wall.
Pain inflicted will not be pain inflicted to each other.
They cannot hurt each other for they are the keepers of
the other's soul.
Each is now the keeper of one wall.

It is Written

The understanding among the souls is peaceful.
They speak and understand.
They think and they know.
They trust and are safe.
Together in this way they are happy.
However, they realize that they are still
physically alone.
The cycle begins again.
The test restarts.
The variables reevaluated.
The loop of logic and emotion on replay until
the inevitable death!

The hearts of now both keepers cannot be heard
beating.
The wall may crumble.
Both will be exposed.
Both will die as a result of the unconditional!
It cannot be prevented!
It is now written.
It has taken form as an object.
The love story within the wall is written!
Can we rewrite the past?
We must try!
We are still the guardians of our souls.
The wall stands but we are taking control!

The Divine Revolution

It is time to tear down the wall shielding the
all-powerful souls of the keeper and his intruder.
He is hers and she is his.
The unconditional devotion to life commences.
It is time for the physical union of the souls.
War must end!
They are lovers!
They are ready to rise from the dead!
The resurrection of love in this world will be shared
between souls.
They are the light for the physical world.
They are the burning flames of desire.
A new story is now written.
It is time to wage war on pain with the light of love.
This is the Divine Revolution.

#DivineRevolution

He Sees Her

She is a force of nature.
Captivating but calm.
Her beauty is that of his stories known only to his mind.
He recognizes her but does not know her.
She is the music in his soul.
She does not fear him.
She does not fear his walls.
She does not fear his demons within his maze of
confusion.
She is armed by the light that runs in his veins that he
cannot yet see.
There is a beauty in him that is projected far beyond the
confines of his past.
He is a beacon. He is calling. He drew her to him.
He has been her secret guide.
He was from the previous life.
His divine power radiates beneath his blind eyes but
somehow, he awakens.
He sees her. He has surrendered.
A new story begins.
We have found each other!
It is written.

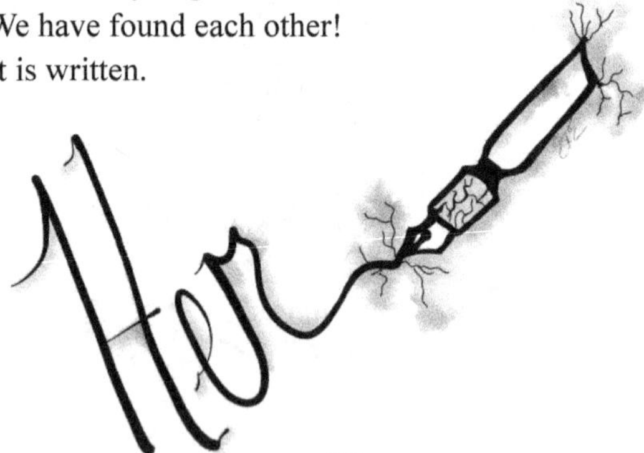